YOUR STARTER HOME PLAYBOOK

A BEGINNER'S GUIDE TO HOMEOWNERSHIP

K. Beck

Copyright © 2024 **K. Beck**

All rights reserved.

PREFACE

This book's content intends solely to assist, not definitively direct your personal, home-buying journey. While I aim to deliver a comprehensive overview, the information presented reflects general guidelines, not tailored counsel. Your route remains unique. Therefore, in addition to reviewing this book, please be sure to take the time before house hunting formally begins to consult applicable specialists actively. You will want to meet with trusted advisors - your chosen attorney, financial planner, experienced loan officer, real estate agent, or other qualified personnel familiar with your background. Discuss specifics like budget projections after candidly detailing your current status, so together you can map a path aligned foremost with your needs. This proactive step allows professionals to consider wider implications and opportunities that broad suggestions here may not capture, empowering you to then make fully informed, confident decisions for your home and household that I cannot match. Please use this as a friendly flashlight, not final authority along a road still unfolding just for you.

DISCLAIMER

Legal Notice: The information provided in this book is for educational and informational purposes only. It is not intended as legal or investment advice or professional guidance. Readers are encouraged to consult with licensed real estate professionals, financial advisors, and legal experts for specific advice tailored to their individual circumstances. The author, as a licensed real estate professional, shares knowledge and insights based on experience and research, but makes no guarantees regarding the accuracy, completeness, or applicability of the information provided. The author and publisher shall not be held liable for any losses, damages, or legal repercussions resulting from the use or interpretation of the information contained in this book. Any reliance on the material presented is at the reader's own risk.

INTRODUCTION

Welcome to the incredible journey of buying your first home! As an author and seasoned real estate agent who has both purchased several homes over the years and guided countless clients through the process, I understand the whirlwind of excitement and uncertainty this major life event brings. I hope that this book serves as your friendly and informative guide every step of the way—from getting financially prepared to making an offer to the final ownership transition. This reader-friendly guide is meant to empower you to navigate one of life's biggest adventures with greater clarity and confidence.

First, let's talk about mindset. For many people, renting is the default option. The main benefits of renting include flexibility, affordability, and less responsibility. But if you want to own a home, you will need to start thinking like a homeowner. This means being willing to commit to a mortgage, taking on the responsibility of maintaining a property, and being prepared for the unexpected costs of homeownership.

Next, you will want to start envisioning yourself as a homeowner. What type of home do you want? What neighborhood do you want to live in? How many bedrooms and bathrooms do you need? Which amenities are important to you? You can start researching once you have a good idea of what you want. Learn about the different types of mortgages available and the costs associated with homeownership. Talk to homeowners you know and ask them about their experiences. What do they love about homeownership? What challenges have they faced?

Once properly prepared, you will be ready to begin the fun part; house-hunting. We'll cover online search tools and the benefits of viewing options in person. We'll also explore different types of home listings and discuss some perks that new construction can offer. You'll discover things you may want to consider when evaluating potential neighborhoods, properties, and floor plans to match your unique lifestyle.

Ready to get serious? We will discuss the bidding and negotiation process as well as why it's important to keep emotionally calm amidst bidding wars and rejected offers. Depending on the market, you may end up submitting a few or possibly several offers before one gets accepted. With the right approach, you will be able to buy your dream starter home without letting stress and uncertainty take over while staying within your budget.

Once an offer is accepted, the real work starts! We will cover the next steps like home inspections, mortgage loan underwriting, and final walkthroughs. Upon completion of this book, you will have developed a clear understanding of the general steps of the entire process. Last-minute surprises won't have to steer your homebuying journey off course.

Once you do secure a home, the journey won't be completely over yet. As a successful new homeowner, establishing solid routines and budgets ensures your property aligns with your greatest hopes rather than becoming a financial drain. By the end, my hope is that you will have gained priceless knowledge and possibly your very own home to show for it.

OVERVIEW

Making the decision to purchase your first home is a significant step that carries both financial and emotional weight. The homebuying process can be complex and overwhelming, particularly for those new to the real estate market. However, by breaking down each step into manageable tasks and approaching them diligently, you can navigate the journey with greater ease and reduced stress. In the upcoming chapters, we will delve into each stage in detail, beginning with a comprehensive overview of the entire process. It's important to note that this book focuses primarily on homebuyers who engage the services of a real estate agent for their home search and are seeking mortgage financing rather than cash purchases. While there may be similarities between the two methods, this book will concentrate on guiding you through the process of securing financing for your ideal home.

1. **Get pre-approved for a mortgage loan**: This initial step should kick off your home-buying journey. Meeting with a lender early on to begin the pre-approval process will give you a clear idea of how much you can borrow, streamlining your entire home-buying experience. Your lender will require details on your income, debts, and assets to provide the preapproval.
2. **Connect with a licensed real estate agent**: A good realtor will help you find homes that fit your needs and budget. They'll also negotiate on your behalf and guide you through the closing process. It's essential to choose someone experienced, knowledgeable, and trustworthy when choosing a real estate agent.
3. **Search for homes:** You can search online, attend open houses, and drive around neighborhoods of interest to look for homes on the market. When you find a home or homes you want to view, your real estate agent will set up appointments,

direct any of your questions about the house to the seller's agent, and more.

4. **Make an offer:** If you find a home you want to buy, you will make an offer to the seller, which your real estate agent will submit on your behalf. The offer should include the purchase price, the amount of earnest money deposit, the proposed closing date, and other contingencies. The seller can accept, reject, or counter all or part of the offer terms. If the seller accepts your offer and signs the purchase contract, you will be officially under contract.

5. **Schedule a home inspection:** Once under contract, you will want to schedule a home inspection with a licensed home inspector. The purpose is to identify any major problems with the home that need to be addressed/repaired. If the home inspection reveals any major problems, you may be able to negotiate with the seller to repair or receive a credit for the repair.

6. **Obtain appraisal results from your lender:** The lender will require an appraisal to ensure the home is worth the purchase price. The appraisal will also help the lender to determine how much money to lend you. Depending on the area, your lender will likely order the appraisal on your behalf.

7. **Obtain home-owner insurance:** You must obtain homeowners insurance before closing the home. Homeowners insurance will protect you from financial loss if the home is damaged or destroyed. Most, if not all, lenders will require you to have this before they can offer you a mortgage loan.

8. **Close on the loan and home purchase:** The closing on the loan and the finalization of your home purchase mark the last leg of the home-buying journey. Before closing, you'll conduct a final walkthrough of the property with your real estate agent to verify all is well. Following this, you'll proceed to the closing meeting to sign the mortgage papers (often with the aid of your attorney or another representative), as well as pay

the down payment and closing costs. Once the loan funds are dispersed, your loan and property purchase are officially "closed," and you'll be handed the keys to your new home!

Table of Contents

Chapter 1: Preparation Is Key 1
    Mindset Shift-From Renter to Homeowner 2
    Budgeting Adequately for Down Payment & Closing Costs 3
    Repairing Credit Issues 4
    Loan Qualification Process 5
    Using Technology/Apps to Assist 9

Chapter 2: The Hunt Begins! 11
    The Role of Real Estate Agents 12
    Defining Your Must-Haves 13
    Evaluating Neighborhoods 15
    Interested In New Construction? 20
    Understanding Various Listing Types 21

Chapter 3: Ready to Make an Offer? 27
    Reading The Market 28
    Negotiation Do's and Don'ts 31

Chapter 4: Your Offer Was Accepted and You Are Under Contract-What's Next? .. 34
    Earnest Money And Escrow 35
    Home Inspection 36

Chapter 5: The Final Walkthrough & Closing 40
    Conducting a Final Walkthrough 41
    Preparing for a Smooth Closing Process 42
    Tips for a Stress-Free Move 43

Chapter 6: Owning With Ease 45
    First Projects to Tackle 46
    Ongoing Maintenance and More 47
    Building Equity Over Time 48
    Key Terms 51
    Navigating Real Estate Transactions Across the 50 States 58

Chapter 1: Preparation Is Key

Mindset Shift-From Renter to Homeowner

Making the switch from renter to homeowner involves a shift in your mindset and approach towards housing expenses. While renting may involve making monthly payments without much consideration for long-term gains, owning a home offers the opportunity to build equity over time. Instead of rent payments lining a landlord's pockets, your mortgage payments contribute to ownership and potential property appreciation. Understanding this shift is crucial for effective budgeting and recognizing your new expenses as investments in long-term financial growth.

If you are struggling with the decision to rent or buy a home, it may be helpful to research average home price appreciation trends over the past several years in your areas of interest. It's common to see property values increase steadily over time, potentially offering significant returns. Knowing homeownership can pay dividends down the line can help ease anxieties over possible higher, upfront costs compared to renting. It's all about changing your perspective from short-term renter to long-term investor in your residence and future financial security.

Another key mindset shift involves accepting the fact that the property you purchase might not have everything you want or look exactly how you have imagined your first home would look. Budgeting for additional costs of future repairs or renovations you want to make is part of homeownership. Very few properties check every box so it's good practice for first time buyers (or any buyer on a budget) to focus first on the structural, safety elements of a home (we will discuss professional home inspections later on). At some point, you may have heard someone say "the house needs updating but has good bones". This is what we are referring to here. You can always make cosmetic upgrades in phases as budgets allow. Think of it as putting together a visual mood board - great bones first, then slowly personalizing with your decor stamps over the months and years ahead.

Budgeting Adequately for Down Payment & Closing Costs

Saving for a down payment and closing costs is often the biggest hurdle for first-time homebuyers. However, with smart budgeting and planning, it is achievable. Start by setting a realistic goal for your down payment amount. This will usually be between 3.5% and 20% of the purchase price (this can vary significantly, depending on the loan product). The higher your down payment, the lower your monthly mortgage payments will be.

Next, create a detailed budget that tracks your income and expenses. This will help you identify areas where you can cut back and save money. There are many budgeting apps and tools available to help you get started. Once you have a budget in place, stick to it! Automate your savings by setting up a recurring transfer from your checking account to your savings account each month. This way, you won't even miss the money you're saving.

In addition to your down payment, you'll also need to budget for closing costs. These expenses, usually between 2% to 5% of the purchase price, cover items such as loan origination fees, appraisal fees, attorney fees, and title insurance. It's important to factor these costs into your budget to avoid any surprises during the closing process. Lastly, remember to consider the additional expenses of homeownership, such as property taxes, insurance, and maintenance.

These costs can fluctuate depending on the location and condition of the home, so it's important to do your research before making an offer. Additionally, several down payment assistance programs are available to help first-time homebuyers. These programs can provide grants or low-interest loans to help cover the cost of a down payment. To determine if you qualify for these programs, ask your mortgage lender to explain them, or you may contact your local housing authority for information.

Repairing Credit Issues

If you have less-than-perfect credit, don't despair. There are ways to improve your credit score before applying for a mortgage. Start by obtaining a free copy of your credit report from each of the three major credit bureaus. * Carefully review your reports for any errors or inaccuracies. If you find any, dispute them immediately. You can also improve your credit score by paying down existing debt, reducing your credit utilization, and making all your payments on time.

It's important to start repairing your credit as early as possible, as it takes time to see a significant improvement in your score. If you are looking to buy a home sooner than later, there are measures you can take to enhance your appeal as a borrower to lenders. Consider securing a co-signer with a strong credit history or opting for a credit builder(secured) loan, tailored to assist individuals with less-than-ideal credit in boosting their scores.

Suggestions to improve your credit score:

- Pay down your debt as quickly as possible.
- Make all of your payments on time.
- Keep your credit utilization low.
- Don't open too many new credit accounts in a short period.
- Consider getting a credit builder loan or secured loan.
- Dispute any errors or inaccuracies on your credit report.

Boosting your credit score requires dedication and patience, yet the rewards can be significant. By following these suggestions, you can increase the likelihood of securing approval for a mortgage loan and potentially qualifying for a lower interest rate.

Finally, remember that credit scores are not the only factor lenders consider when approving a mortgage. They will also examine your income, employment history, and debt-to-income ratio. So, even if your credit score is not perfect, you may still be able to get approved for a mortgage if you have a strong financial history in other areas.

If you find you need additional help with building up your credit, a credit counselor might be a good option. You can search for credit counselors online or you can ask your mortgage lender if they can recommend some.

Loan Qualification Process

The loan qualification process involves providing detailed information to a lender regarding your financial picture, including income, outstanding debts, and assets. The lender will evaluate factors like your credit score and capacity to make monthly mortgage payments. This analysis is used to determine the loan amount and competitive interest rates for which you qualify.

Additionally, understanding the distinction between pre-approval and pre-qualification is crucial for aspiring homebuyers, as one represents a formal commitment from a lender based on detailed financial information, while the other serves as a preliminary estimate with less reliability.

1. **Pre-approval**: A pre-approval is a formal commitment from a lender to lend you a certain amount of money to purchase a home. To get pre-approved, you must inform the lender about your financial situation, including your income, employment,

and debts. The lender will then review your information to determine how much they will lend you.
2. **Pre-qualification**: A pre-qualification is a less formal estimate of how much you can borrow. A prequalification is typically based on a quick review of your financial information and is less reliable than a pre-approval.

Benefits of getting pre-approved for a mortgage loan include:

You will have a better understanding of your home buying budget. A loan pre-approval lets you know exactly how much a lender is willing to finance so you can shop confidently for homes within your price range.

You can secure financing more quickly. Since the lender has already examined your financial credentials, the loan process moves faster, allowing you to close on a home more rapidly when you're ready to make an offer.

You may qualify for better interest rates. Once the lender reviews your information and loan options, you may qualify for a lower rate than expected.

You become a more attractive buyer to sellers. Pre-approval letters confirm to sellers that your financing is secure, giving you a competitive edge over buyers who haven't taken this step. Most sellers prefer buyers who have been pre-qualified by a reputable lender.

The loan preapproval process typically takes a few days up to a couple of weeks (this can vary significantly based on the lender and individual buyer circumstances). Some of the documents typically required by your lender for the preapproval are as follows:

- Pay stubs from the past two months

- W-2 forms from the past two years
- Tax returns from the past two years
- Bank statements from the past two months
- Investment account statements
- Retirement account statements
- Proof of other income, such as child support or alimony

Keep in mind that the above is not an exhaustive list. Depending on your personal circumstances, you may be required to submit more documents than what is listed here. Once your lender has all of the necessary information, they will review all and determine if you qualify for a mortgage loan. If so, they will issue you a loan pre-approval letter. This letter states the maximum amount of money you can borrow and/or the maximum purchase price of property you are qualified to buy. It is important to note that a pre-approval letter does not guarantee a loan. The final loan approval (which occurs at the latter end of the process) will depend on several factors, including the appraisal of the home and your continued financial stability.

Additional tips regarding the loan pre-approval process: Gather all required documents beforehand, be transparent about your financial status with your lender, and prioritize getting pre-approved before beginning your home search.

Which Loan Type Is Right for You?

Traditional Loans Vs. Special Loan Programs:

1. **Traditional loans**: Traditional loans are the most common type of mortgage. They are available from banks, credit unions, and other lenders. Traditional loans typically have fixed interest rates, which means that the interest rate will stay the same for the life of the loan. This can provide peace of

mind, as you will know exactly how much your monthly mortgage payments will be.
2. **Special loan programs**: Some special loan programs help first-time homebuyers and other borrowers who may not qualify for a traditional loan. These programs typically have more flexible credit and income requirements than traditional loans and may offer lower interest rates.

Some of the most common special loan programs include:

- **FHA loans:** FHA loans are insured by the Federal Housing Administration (FHA). This makes them less risky for lenders, which allows them to offer lower interest rates and more flexible credit requirements. FHA loans require a minimum down payment of 3.5%.
- **VA loans:** VA loans are available to active-duty military members, veterans, and spouses. VA loans do not require a down payment and have competitive interest rates.
- **USDA loans:** USDA loans are available to borrowers purchasing homes in rural areas. USDA loans do not require a down payment and have competitive interest rates.

The best type of loan for you will depend on your financial situation and goals. If you have good credit and a stable income, you may be able to qualify for a traditional loan. You may want to consider a special loan program if you have less-than-perfect credit or a lower income.

Additional things to consider when choosing a loan:

- **Down payment amount:** The size of your down payment will affect the amount of money that you need to borrow and the amount of your monthly mortgage payments.

- **Interest rate:** The interest rate on your loan will determine how much you will pay in interest over the life of the loan.
- **Loan terms:** This will determine how long you have to repay the loan and how much your monthly mortgage payments will be.

It is important to talk to a lender to get more information about the different types of loans/special programs available and to find the best loan for your needs. Finally, remember that the loan qualification process is not just about getting approved. It's also an opportunity to learn more about your financial situation and make sure that you are making informed decisions about your home purchase.

I have witnessed many buyers delaying getting preapproved for a mortgage loan until they find a property. In doing so, they often have missed out on having their offer considered because sellers will usually prefer to work with a buyer that is already preapproved. I always strongly suggest that buyers start with the preapproval process before looking at properties. It can help avoid delays and disappointments later on. There is usually an expiration date on these, but if your preapproval letter does expire, you can contact the lender that issued it, and they should be able to quickly generate an updated copy (assuming none of your original information has changed). If it has, let your lender know and they can make any necessary adjustments.

Using Technology/Apps to Assist

Technology has made the homebuying process easier and more efficient than ever before. Many useful apps and tools help you budget, save for a down payment, and find the right home.

1. **Budgeting apps:** There are many budgeting apps available that can help you track your income and expenses. At the time of this writing, some popular budgeting apps include Mint, YNAB, and PocketGuard. These apps can help you create a

budget, track your spending, and identify areas where you can save money.
2. **Savings apps:** Several apps can help you save money for a down payment. At the time of this writing, some popular savings apps include Acorns, Personal Capital, and Stash. These apps can help you set savings goals, automate your savings, and invest your money.
3. **Home search apps:** Many home search apps can help you find homes for sale in your desired area. Some popular home search apps include Zillow, Trulia, and Realtor.com. These apps allow you to search for homes by price, location, and other criteria. You can also view photos and videos of the homes and read reviews from other buyers.
4. **Mortgage calculators:** Several mortgage calculators are available that can help you estimate your monthly mortgage payments. This can help determine how much you can afford to borrow. You can find mortgage calculators on the websites of banks, credit unions, and other lenders.

In addition to these apps and tools, several online resources can help you with homebuying. For example, the Consumer Financial Protection Bureau (CFPB) offers several resources for first-time homebuyers, including a step-by-step guide to the homebuying process.

You may obtain a free credit report from each of the three main credit reporting agencies, Equifax, Experian, and TransUnion, once a year by going to AnnualCreditReport.com. This is the only approved source for free credit reports under federal law. Keep in mind that these reports do not offer credit ratings, but they do allow you to evaluate your credit history, look for errors, and watch for potential symptoms of identity theft.

Chapter 2: The Hunt Begins!

The Role of Real Estate Agents

When you're ready to start looking for a home, you will want to enlist the help of an experienced, knowledgeable, and trustworthy real estate agent. A good agent can make homebuying much easier and less stressful. They will guide you step by step so there are no surprises as you move forward. Below are just a few of the services a real estate agent provides:

- Find homes that meet your needs. This can be done by setting up a search in the Multiple Listing Service, and listings are typically emailed to you in real-time, daily, weekly, etc.
- Schedule showings- Your agent needs to be available when you are to view homes.
- Negotiate the best possible price based on recent sales of similar properties.
- Provide referrals to licensed and reviewed service partners (lenders, inspectors, attorneys etc.)

Things to consider when searching for a real estate agent:

- Ask for recommendations from friends, family, co-workers, etc.
- Search online for agents in your area. Read reviews when available.
- Interview several agents before making a decision.
- Ask about their experience, knowledge, and fees.
- Choose an agent whom you feel comfortable with and who you trust.

In addition to these responsibilities, a reliable real estate agent can offer valuable advice and support at every stage of the homebuying journey. They assist in navigating the local market, making informed decisions, and help you steer clear of potential pitfalls. A committed agent will be accessible through phone, text, and email, even during evenings and weekends as they recognizing that homebuying often extends beyond conventional business hours.

One way to ensure you have a knowledgeable and ethical agent on your side is to confirm that they are a Realtor®. The term Realtor® is a registered trademark that refers to a real estate agent who is an active member of the National Association of Realtors® (NAR). Realtors® must complete extensive training, adhere to a strict code of ethics, and have access to the latest market data and resources. Working with a Realtor® means you'll have someone who is committed to protecting your best interests and providing the highest level of service throughout your home buying journey.

A real estate agent may have a buyer client sign a Buyer Representation Agreement or Exclusive Buyer Representation Agreement before working with them. This agreement outlines the agent's responsibilities, the buyer's obligations, and the terms of their working relationship. It establishes the agent as the buyer's representative and typically includes details on commission, duration of the agreement, and the agent's fiduciary duties to the buyer. Signing this agreement helps clarify expectations, protect the buyer's interests, and ensure a smoother real estate transaction process.

Defining Your Must-Haves

Before you start looking at listings, take a few minutes to jot down what you absolutely need in a home, what you'd like to have but can be flexible on, and what would be a definite deal-breaker. This will help you focus your search on homes that best match your requirements.

Start by listing out all of your most desired features such as the number of bedrooms and bathrooms, kitchen size and type, outdoor space, proximity to transportation, and whatever else you have on your most-wanted list. Also, consider any future needs such as room for a growing family or space for visiting guests. Next, group these features into three categories:

1. Must-Haves-things you cannot compromise on, such as sufficient number of bedrooms to accommodate all occupants, specific school district, garage, etc.
2. Would-Like-to-Have-nice to have items that you can be flexible with such as extra bedrooms or rec room, extra storage space, high-end appliances, finished basement, etc.
3. Deal Breakers- things that are definite no-gos, such as long and complicated commutes, not enough storage to accommodate your needs, no basement, etc.

Once you have your wish-list sorted, you will want to work out a realistic budget. Consider all your expenses to determine what you can comfortably afford each month and in the long run.

Keep in mind, it's important to be flexible and open-minded during your home search. You may fall in love with a home that doesn't meet all of your must-haves. If this happens, weigh the pros and cons carefully before deciding whether to pursue it or move on. You may be willing to compromise on some of your wants if the home is otherwise perfect for you. Also, consider the fact that this is your first home and that you may upgrade to a different home in the future. You might compromise on certain wishlist items for now, with the understanding that they could be achievable in your next home.

Evaluating Neighborhoods

When you are prepared to attend property viewings, or even before if you have specific locations in mind, it's beneficial to conduct some research on the neighborhoods you're interested in. This research may involve examining factors like crime rates, school districts, local amenities, and other relevant details. It's essential for homebuyers to take the initiative to thoroughly investigate the areas they are considering. ** Note-The Federal Fair Housing Act safeguards homebuyers from housing discrimination and imposes limitations on the actions and communications of real estate agents. (see below for more information regarding Federal Fair Housing Act)*

Below are some factors to consider when evaluating a neighborhood:

- **Crime-rate:** You can find crime statistics for most neighborhoods online.
- **School district:** If you have children or plan to have children in the future, you'll want to consider the quality of the schools in the area. You can find school ratings online.
- **Amenities:** Consider the amenities that are important to you. Do you want to be close to shops, restaurants, and public transportation? Do you prefer a more secluded neighborhood?
- **Home values:** You'll also want to consider the home values in the area. To ensure you are buying a home in an area with stable or rising values, ask your real estate agent to provide a Comparative Market Analysis Report for your area(s) of interest.

- **Atmosphere:** The overall atmosphere of a neighborhood is also important to consider. Do you want to live in a quiet, family-friendly neighborhood? Do you prefer a more vibrant, urban neighborhood? It can also be very helpful to visit the neighborhoods you're considering at different times and days of the week. This will give you a better sense of the neighborhood's atmosphere and whether or not it's a good fit for you. It helps to ask yourself, "Can I picture myself living here?"

Finding a house that feels like home means visualizing not just the property as it is but envisioning it as the backdrop for your future life. Think about the activities you enjoy, how you entertain friends or unwind after work, and how a home can support your lifestyle.

As you tour properties, consider whether the spaces adapt to your needs. Can the living room accommodate your weekly book club meetings or game nights? Is there a peaceful spot for you to work or pursue hobbies? Imagine hosting holidays, having family stay over, or where you might plant your first garden.

Pay attention to how the flow and function of the home feel as you walk through it. Remember that small aesthetic changes are easy, but structural changes come with significant costs and time. Therefore, thinking beyond paint colors or carpet styles is crucial to the underlying features and layout.

Think long-term as well. Will the home suit your needs as your family or career grows? Is there flexibility in the space for anticipated lifestyle changes, whether it's a new baby, a home business, or downsizing once children leave the nest?

Exploring Various Property Types

If you are unsure whether a single-family home or an attached home is the right fit for you, another factor to consider before starting your home search is familiarizing yourself with the different property types in the areas you are considering. Each has its own advantages and drawbacks, such as size, amenities, and maintenance needs

1. **Single Family Homes**- These stand-alone houses are the most popular alternative and come in a variety of forms such as ranch, split-level, two-story, and more. While typically the most costly, they provide the greatest privacy and room for the money, as there are no shared walls. The homeowner is responsible for the maintenance of the exterior and yard. *Note that some single-family homes may still belong to a Homeowners Association (HOA), which could impose additional rules and fees on the property.*
2. **Townhomes/Townhouses**- These homes provide a connected housing alternative with shared walls between units. You retain ownership of the internal area as well as limited exterior areas. Townhomes occur in a variety of layouts and sizes, and upkeep of shared spaces is typically handled by a homeowners' organization.
3. **Condominiums- Condos**- Often known as connected living spaces, are primarily apartment-style units that are owned independently. The unit interiors are private, while common areas like as lobbies, fitness centers, and parking garages are shared. Monthly condo association fees cover the cost of maintaining common areas and building exteriors.
4. **Cooperative Housing**- With a co-op, you effectively own shares in the corporation that owns the building. No mortgage is necessary; instead, you will receive a private lease for your unit. Co-op boards thoroughly examine purchasers and impose stringent rules on renovations and rents. Maintenance and property taxes are included in monthly carrying expenses.

These are often available in big urban areas such as New York, Chicago, and San Francisco.

In addition to single-family detached homes, attached housing options such as condos, co-ops and townhouses offer first-time buyers more affordable options with shared upkeep. Evaluate tradeoffs like size, amenities and community rules as you explore alternatives to standalone houses that best fit your needs and lifestyle.

Comparing Online Listings to In-Person Home Searches

Browsing through popular real estate platforms like Trulia and Zillow provides the convenience of exploring homes on the market from the comfort of your own home. With just a few clicks, you can narrow down listings based on location, price, bedrooms, amenities, and more. However, while these online tools offer ease, it's beneficial to complement your digital research with in-person home tours.

While searching on sites such as Trulia or Zillow, you're limited to facts and photos, viewing a property in person grants you a deeper insight that digital listings can't capture. You can assess intricate details like lighting, storage space, layout flow, and craftsmanship. Factors such as the overall look, neighborhood ambiance, and noise levels are best evaluated during an on-site visit.

Engaging in live property searches allows for a more profound emotional connection. While online listings provide a general idea of a home, physically walking through the space often evokes instinctive reactions that reveal whether the property truly resonates with you. Virtual platforms and restricted open houses may cause you to overlook hidden treasures or misjudge spaces that may not photograph well but possess potential.

Ultimately, striking a balance between online screening and physical walkthroughs allows homebuyers to maximize technology while making deeply personal purchasing decisions. When assessing your choices, I would suggest that you prioritize viewing properties in person whenever feasible. This approach offers the most comprehensive perspective on the homes you're considering, empowering you to make informed and confident decisions.

Things to consider while touring homes:

- Have your agent schedule all appointments in advance, grouping showings efficiently.
- Arrive on time and come prepared with a notebook to record notes about each property.
- Expect to remove shoes.
- Assess the condition of floors, walls, fixtures, and systems mindfully.
- Ask your agent to forward your questions about the home to the seller's agent.
- Refrain from rushed decisions under pressure. Only make an offer on properties you are sure about. This may change depending on the current market. In a market with multiple offers being the norm, you may want to submit an offer right away.

Prospective buyers who are house hunting remotely across states or while abroad may choose to authorize a designated representative to access listings on their behalf through their real estate agent. They can grant permission formally to their agent via email. The buyer's agent would then accompany the chosen stand-in during all showings to provide home details or highlights for later discussion with the buyer over the phone, video, or via email.

Interested In New Construction?

As first-time homebuyers, choosing between buying new construction or an existing dwelling proves a significant decision with long-term lifestyle and financial implications.

While existing and/or older homes offer established neighborhoods, floorplans, and the ability to move in promptly after closing, newer homes provide extensive customization during building alongside modern construction standards and cutting-edge amenities.

Weighing the pros and cons helps determine the ideal fit. Here's an overview of key reasons why you may prefer purchasing new construction:

Personalized Design Input

Depending on the builder, buyers may be provided the opportunity to meet with design consultants to customize floorplans to fit their family needs and lifestyle. More buyer choices may include exterior elevations, cabinetry finishes, lighting schemas, smart home tech integrations, and structural layout. Each builder will vary in terms of which features and to what extent a buyer can customize.

Latest Styles & Fixtures

New construction utilizes modern architecture aesthetics on home exteriors compared to dated styles of existing homes that were built decades ago. Clean sightlines, statement windows, and on-trend landscaping are some examples. Home interiors typically provide open concept living with finishes such as contemporary countertops, cabinets and flooring, typically included in baseline pricing. With new construction, buyers can expect contemporary lighting fixtures and appliances as well.

Adding to the appeal, buyers whose budgets allow can pay more for additional, higher-end upgrades if desired.

Energy Efficient Materials

Thanks to evolving building codes, many recently built homes incorporate cutting-edge construction methods and materials that maximize energy efficiency, potentially saving new owners thousands in future utility costs. For example, high-performance triple pane windows, additional wall/roof insulation, LED lighting, tankless water heaters, and zoned HVAC systems optimize heating, cooling, and electrical usage throughout all living spaces. Programmable smart home hubs facilitate remote appliance control as well.

Customized Outdoor Oasis

Apart from the main house itself, in newly constructed neighborhoods, buyers often have the opportunity to personalize their outdoor areas as well. Depending on the builder and location, you might be able to add features such as built-in patios, fireplaces, outdoor kitchens with ample prep areas and storage, or amenities like pools and spas. Skilled landscaping teams can transform your ideas into reality by creating beautiful gardens and laying down fresh sod.

While there are many great options for existing homes on the market, new construction opens doors for buyers seeking modern home design input, upgraded features, and energy efficiencies packaged from a single point of accountability. Getting in early on pre/new construction can allow for maximum customization for buyers.

Understanding Various Listing Types

As you start your home search, you'll encounter different listing classifications that provide insights into a property's status and ownership. Understanding these distinctions is essential for making informed decisions, especially when considering an unfamiliar listing type like a short sale. Here is an overview of the various listing types you may encounter while exploring your options:

Regular Sale

Sellers commonly partner with a real estate agent to officially list the home through the regional Multiple Listing Service (MLS) database accessible to all area agents. This exposes the home to maximum buyer audiences. The listed price should reflect the current fair market value based on recent comparable sales and home attributes. Typically, buyers submit purchase offers (most often their real estate agent submits the offer on buyer's behalf) directly to the seller's agent, who negotiates on seller's behalf. Standard contingencies around financing, appraisal, and inspections prevail.

Private Network

Some sellers opt for private listings before going public with their sale. These "pocket listings" may omit specific addresses or property details when entered into the MLS database. Only other agents can access this information, and the listing should indicate whether agents can share it with their clients. Sellers may choose private listings to avoid attracting unqualified buyers or to have time to prepare before hitting the market. Apart from confidentiality, private listings operate similarly to regular sale listings in terms of offers and price negotiation.

In a seller's market, when inventory is limited, having your real estate agent be on top of private listings as soon as they are available can be crucial and a huge benefit for a buyer. It may provide less competition against other buyers and a possibility of getting a better price for the home if a bidding war is avoided. As an agent, I always check the private listing network (PLN) for my clients' areas of interest. I have been able to help numerous buyers purchase a home while still listed in the private network in areas where properties are scarce. Be sure to let your agent know you want to be informed of private and public listings when you start your home search. Keep in mind, for some of the private listings that do not yet allow showing appointments and have no scheduled date to go live, it may help to ask your agent keep any eye on it and/or keep in touch with the seller's agent so that when showings are allowed, you can be one of the first to view the property.

Short Sale

A short sale listing occurs when a homeowner is facing foreclosure and attempts to sell their house for less than the amount outstanding in mortgage loans. With the bank accepting a smaller settlement, owners can escape foreclosure while transferring the troubled property. Short sales, unlike traditional house sales, are subject to lender clearance throughout the negotiating process. The approval requirements and processing durations vary substantially depending on the jurisdiction and bank approach. In slower judicial jurisdictions, such as Florida, some short sales might take 9-12 months to be approved by the bank. Meanwhile, in efficient nonjudicial zones such as Seattle, expedited approvals may occur in as little as one month. Regional foreclosure rules have an influence on short sale timescales, as do individual bank loss mitigation aims. Buyers interested in short sale transactions should consult with their agent to learn about the steps involved, realistic wait periods for bank answers, and other details. Patience is essential while looking for short sale options.

Note-If you have a specific deadline to find and close on a property (i.e. you want to be moved in by the time your lease is up in a few months), pursuing the purchase of a short-sale property may not be ideal due to the uncertain wait time. However, buyers interested in a short-sale property may be able to secure temporary living arrangements or ask their landlord if they will consider a month-to-month lease option while waiting for the process to be finalized.

Foreclosure

In addition to pre-foreclosure ads, purchasers should keep a look out for foreclosed homes. Many of these are listed on the Multiple Listing Service (MLS). These bank-owned residences, also known as REO (Real Estate Owned) properties, have already gone through a foreclosure auction without third-party bidding high enough to cover the overdue mortgage obligation. The foreclosing lender then assumes possession and sells the property at fair market value via traditional MLS or other means. While REO properties sometimes require repairs due to neglect, a lack of utilities, or past owner damage, purchasers can occasionally locate move-in ready distressed homes for less than market value. You can contact your agent or attorney for further information about foreclosures and other things you should know before making an offer on one of these homes.

For Sale by Owner

Homes advertised for sale by owner (FSBO) indicate that the seller is promoting and selling the home without the assistance of an agent. Buyers profit from FSBOs because they have more negotiating power because agency commissions are not factored into pricing. However, without agent assistance, the transaction procedure and the writing of purchase contracts can be challenging. Buyer's agents can help FSBO purchasers by proposing reasonable offer techniques, expediting paperwork, and so forth. While FSBOs may save on commissions, many purchasers continue to use real estate agents for expert guidance while looking for alternative property alternatives.

* Understanding Fair Housing Laws

The Fair home Act of 1968 offers federal protection against discrimination in home transactions. This civil rights act seeks to provide equitable housing opportunities regardless of race, color, national origin, religion, gender, familial situation, or handicap. During real estate transactions, both buyers and sellers must be aware of these restrictions.

Fair housing rules provide you the right to buy, finance, or rent a house in any community without fear of discrimination. For example, a real estate salesperson cannot refuse to show properties in certain communities because the majority of the people are of a specific race or religion. They also cannot deny you a screening because you have small children. Real estate brokers cannot limit your dwelling alternatives by only presenting listings in specific regions with protected features. They must also meet unique requirements relating to a handicap at no additional cost. For example, if you require a wheelchair, they should present model homes with wheelchair accessibility rather than just multilevel residences.

Examples of violations buyers may face include:

- An agent refusing to work with you because you do not speak fluent English. This qualifies as national origin discrimination.
- You apply for an apartment but get denied by the landlord, citing your mental disability as the reason, claiming you could disturb other tenants. This violates disability discrimination protections.
- A lender quotes you a higher mortgage rate due to gender rather than solely assessing your credit qualifications, denying equal opportunity.

If you feel you've been treated unfairly by a real estate or lending pro, you have options. You can file a complaint with the Department of Housing and Urban Development (HUD) or reach out to a fair housing organization for assistance. It's important to keep thorough records—jot down names and notes from all your conversations, and back up any chats with written evidence. These records will help track your

complaint history, showing clearly when and how the discrimination took place.

Chapter 3: Ready to Make an Offer?

Reading The Market

As a first-time homebuyer, being well-prepared and knowledgeable about the bidding process is essential to ensure a successful outcome. First and foremost, it's crucial to understand the importance of timing in the real estate market. Market conditions vary greatly, and knowing the current trends and seasonality can help you decide when to make your offer. For instance, if you're in a seller's market, you may need to be prepared to act quickly and make a competitive offer to secure the property. On the other hand, if you're in a buyer's market, you may have more negotiating power and can potentially secure a better deal.

Buyer's or Seller's Market?

As a soon-to-be first-time homeowner, few factors will have a greater influence on your journey than determining whether we are in a buyers' or sellers' market. The dynamics of housing supply and demand, pricing power, negotiation leverage, and competitiveness are some of the aspects to examine in both scenarios.

In a buyer's market, a large home inventory combined with low demand puts buyers in control. Buyers acquire significant influence over sellers who are anxiously awaiting an offer due to ample inventory and fewer competing bidders. When supply exceeds demand, purchasers are more likely able to negotiate the purchase price, repairs, closing expenses, and other issues with the seller. Expect to see market listings last longer as well.

Historically, mortgage rates tend to drop during buyer's markets, leading to increased buyer purchasing power by enabling them to lock in low monthly payments. Overall, when demand declines and sellers compete for restricted sales, consumers benefit in a variety of ways.

Alternatively, seller's markets demonstrate the other extreme: low inventory meets inflated demand, possibly making it very challenging for buyers to not only find a home in their areas of interest but also to secure a contract. Existing homeowners are hesitant to sell during uncertain times, so fewer properties are put on the market and inventory might be limited. New construction may also lag. These persistent shortages cause purchasers to scramble as newly listed houses attract high demand and offers that may far exceed asking prices. *

Instead of negotiating, buyers in a seller's market are taking a more aggressive approach, such as offering sellers flexible closing date options, waiving protections such as appraisals (if permitted by the buyer's lender), and home inspections to make their offer more competitive with rival bidders. Buyers must also be prepared to move/close fast when making an offer, since houses frequently go under contract rapidly in a seller's market. Any hesitancy on the buyer's behalf might lead to a missed opportunity. Some purchasers may not understand this until they have missed out on a cherished house several times.

While unforeseen forces continuously reconfigure markets, evaluating indicators such as the number of days on the market, month-to-month price variations, and sale-to-list price ratios can help distinguish between the two. Tracking these metrics enables buyers to act decisively when the market swings in their favor. Understanding both possibilities can make the home-buying process much less complex and stressful since you will know what to expect.

Crafting a Competitive Offer

Typically, once you find a property you wish to make an offer on, your agent will gather comparable, recently sold properties within the proximity of the home and provide you with this information. Knowing how much similar properties have sold for will give you an idea of market values and, in turn, approximately how much to offer and how much you will likely end up paying for the home.

When making an offer, there are several factors to consider. These include offer price, terms of the sale, a proposed closing date, and any additional conditions or contingencies you may want to include.

Once you've submitted your offer, it's essential to be prepared for the possibility of a counteroffer from the seller. This may involve adjusting your offer price, revising the terms of the sale, or addressing any concerns the seller may have. It's important to remain flexible and open to negotiation, as this can ultimately lead to a more successful outcome.

During a time when there may be few houses for sale and many eager buyers, you may have to submit offers on multiple homes before one gets accepted by the seller. That's totally normal—it's not about you so don't take it personally and try not to let it bring you down if and when an offer falls through. Look at it as gaining experience that gets you closer to what works. The more you learn about reasonable prices in different areas, the smarter you can negotiate. Keep in mind that finding "the one" is worth the wait, even if it takes touring many homes over a longer period of time. Focus on must-haves without going over-budget just to rush in. Working with your agent to adjust as you go often leads to successful offer acceptance. Stay optimistic and remember that the perfect home for you is out there and each bid helps get your foot in the ownership door if you stick with it.

The Purchase Contract-What Buyers Should Know

A real estate transaction can be complicated, involving contracts, documentation, and significant financial and legal considerations. While real estate agents can complete purchase agreement forms while filling in offer terms to submit to seller, they are not permitted by law to interpret contracts or give legal advice to clients. Having an expert real estate attorney defend your unique interests as a buyer is priceless. An attorney guarantees that your rights are properly protected, advises on ambiguous language in the offer, and negotiates tailored terms and contingencies. They also evaluate crucial papers such as inspection reports to identify flaws, go over the deed to ensure a clear title transfer, and prepare for a smooth closing by examining paperwork to avoid complications. With such high financial stakes involved in a property purchase, a buyer should always hire an attorney rather than risk costly complications without legal skill and guidance. Attorneys protect you when contracts are signed, complex transactions unfold, and large investments are made in one of life's most critical purchases.

Negotiation Do's and Don'ts

Do..

- **Be prepared to walk away from the deal.** This is one of the most important negotiation tips. If the seller is unwilling to negotiate on something that is a deal breaker for you, (for example based on current market statistics you believe the asking price is too high), be prepared to leave the deal. There are other homes out there and you don't want to agree to something you are not comfortable with or that you may regret later.
- **Be willing to compromise on some issues.** You're probably not going to get everything you want in a negotiation. Be willing to compromise on some issues to reach an agreement. For example, you may be willing to pay a little more for the home if the seller is willing to make certain repairs.
- **Be patient and persistent.** The negotiation process can take time. Don't get discouraged if the seller doesn't immediately accept your offer. Being patient and persistent is usually your best chance to reach an agreement.

- **Do your research.** Before you start negotiating, research and find out how much similar homes in the area are selling for (your agent can help you determine this by providing market information). This is an easy and straightforward way to determine a realistic offer price for the home you're interested in.
- **Get everything in writing.** Once you and the seller have agreed on terms, get everything in writing (both parties should sign the contract at this point). This includes the purchase price, the closing costs, the repairs that need to be made, closing date, and any other important terms and agreed upon items.

Don't..

- **Make an offer that you can't afford.** This is a surefire way to get yourself into financial trouble. Make sure you have a clear understanding of your budget before you start negotiating.
- **Be afraid to ask for concessions from the seller.** The seller may be willing to provide some concessions for the closing costs, or some repairs that need to be made. Don't be afraid to ask for what you want. They may or may not agree, but if it's reasonable to the circumstances, it's probably worth it to ask.
- **Don't let your emotions take over during the negotiation process.** It's important to keep your emotions in check during the negotiation process. If you get emotional, you're more likely to overlook the important issues or make an incorrect decision. Remember, the seller may be as nervous and anxious as you and/or may have multiple individuals who have a say in negotiating decisions.
- **Don't rush the process.** The negotiation process can take time. Don't rush the process, or you may make a mistake. Take

your time and ensure you're happy with the terms of the deal before you sign anything.

As a real estate professional assisting many first-time homebuyers, one of the most confusing topics is the expectation to bid over a seller's listing price. "Doesn't the list price reflect what the seller wants/expects for their home?" is a reasonable question from most first-time home-buyers. However, market dynamics have transformed due to limited housing inventory and intense demand – bidding wars have become the new norm in many areas. The role of real estate agents should include informing and educating buyer clients to strategically navigate this situation without overextending their budget.

Chapter 4: Your Offer Was Accepted and You Are Under Contract-What's Next?

Earnest Money And Escrow

Earnest money is a deposit you pay to establish your serious intent to buy a property. It is usually a minor portion of the overall house price. When your purchase offer is accepted, the earnest money you pay is stored in an escrow account run by a neutral third party, such as a title agency, seller's (or buyer's) real estate brokerage, or an attorney. This earnest money deposit is normally applied to your final payment at closing. It's important to recognize that earnest money and escrow play distinct functions. Earnest money is a personal deposit. The term "escrow" refers to a third-party account that securely keeps payments during the buying process.

The escrow service plays a crucial role in protecting both the buyer and the seller throughout the transaction. In the event that either party fails to fulfill their obligations as outlined in the contract, earnest money may either be returned to the buyer or forfeited and transferred to the seller, depending on the specific circumstances and contract contingencies.

Given the legal and financial consequences, it's recommended that buyers consult with their real estate attorney about earnest money amounts, escrow services, and purchase contract conditions before making an offer.

Attorney Review Period- In states such as New Jersey and Illinois, e.g., it is a standard practice to have a designated period, typically around 3 to 5 business days, for buyers and sellers to have their attorneys review the terms of the contract before it becomes legally binding. This is referred to as the "attorney review" period, which allows for legal scrutiny, modifications, and necessary adjustments to the agreement to protect the interests of both parties involved in the transaction.

Home Inspection

Understanding The Home Inspection Process

Once the buyer's offer is accepted by the seller and they are officially under contract, they will want to schedule a professional home inspection. This usually occurs within a few days after contract acceptance, unless the purchase agreement stipulates a different schedule.

The goal of the inspection is to assess the physical condition of the entire property prior to making a purchase official. Homebuyers should hire a qualified, licensed professional home inspector to visually assess items such as the roof, foundation, walls, electrical systems, plumbing, HVAC, appliances, drainage, and more. The inspector searches for major cracks, leaks, defective functioning, and components that may need to be changed due to age or wear.

It's a good idea for buyers to reach out to a few different home inspection companies to inquire about the scope of their services, associated prices, certificates, and so on. Some may charge extra for further testing for mold, lead paint, radon, or sewer scoping. Buyers should confirm in advance that the inspector is licensed to work in the area where the subject property is located.

Inspectors can analyze obvious abnormalities, but they cannot diagnose or prescribe repairs because they are not qualified contractors. Their reports describe areas of concern and weaknesses based on their professional experience. When problems beyond their scope, they usually recommend purchasers to competent professionals such as an HVAC technician, plumber, or electrician for additional inspection.

Ultimately, the goal of a home inspection is to educate purchasers of apparent repairs that are required as well as potential concerns. If faults are discovered, purchasers might attempt to negotiate credits or fixes with sellers using the purchase contract conditions. Being proactive in understanding what a home inspection comprises helps that purchasers get the most out of this beneficial procedure.

Complete the Loan Application

The mortgage application process begins with acquiring all essential papers the lender needs to move forward. If you had previously submitted the items below during the initial pre-approval process, your lender will most likely want updated copies of some documents. Typical required documents include:

- Government-issued ID.
- W-2s and tax returns (last two years)
- Pay stubs (last two months)
- Bank statements (last two months)
- Statements for investment and retirement accounts.
- Additional income verification (Social Security benefits, child support, etc.)
- A signed purchase agreement

Depending on your financial status, certain lenders may require additional documentation to what is listed here. Providing complete and precise documents in a timely manner can expedite the processing of your loan application.

Once you have all of your paperwork ready, the loan officer will assist you in filling out the full application, which includes your income, spending, assets, debts, credit history, and other information. Answering completely ensures that your lender gets a clear picture when evaluating your eligibility for mortgage financing. Discuss any questions or concerns you have with your lender as they occur.

Staying organized and responsive throughout the paperwork process will ensure that everything runs well, even with the flurry of details that come with buying a new property. You will want to immediately inform your lender of any changes to your finances or situation to avoid delays in processing and/or the contract closing date.

Additional Key Steps in the Mortgage Process:

1. **Appraisal** - The lender requires an impartial appraiser to determine if the contract price accurately reflects the property's current fair market value. This contributes to funding the loan amount. Appraisals are typically ordered immediately after a signed purchase agreement and may take up to a few weeks to complete. If the appraisal determines the property's' assessed value is less than the contract amount, the lender may deny the loan until or unless the price is renegotiated.

2. **Interest Rate Lock** - When applicable, you might choose to lock in an interest rate for a set length of time to safeguard against market fluctuations. This ensures the rate given by your lender for 30 to 60 days. Consult with your lender to see if locking in makes sense given current rate trends.

3. **Underwriting** - Underwriters thoroughly review all income sources, assets, debts, and credit data on mortgage applications to ensure borrowers can meet their commitments. You should avoid making major purchases that will affect your credit score or debt-to-income ratios until after closing, since these changes may prevent loan approval.

4. **Closing** -The final step before receiving mortgage money is to sign final loan paperwork and pay closing costs/down payment. This makes the loan official because the property and title are transferred to you.

Staying in touch with your lender throughout these steps ensures a smooth transition from borrower to homeowner. They can guide you on final requirements leading up to closing day.

Securing the Best Mortgage Rates:

Interest rates have a substantial influence on mortgage expenses. Lower rates mean lower monthly payments and longer-term savings. Suggestions to help ensure you secure the best rate include:

• **Shop Around Extensively** - Compare quotes from different lenders before choosing the first rate given. Checking rates online and in person provides you more negotiation power via competition.

• **Consider Shorter Loan Terms** - Although monthly payments are greater, shorter periods (e.g., 15 years vs 30 years) can significantly lower overall interest paid throughout the life of the loan. Determine if you can afford greater monthly payments for long-term investments.

• **Buy Discount Points** - Paying discount points (usually 1% of the total loan amount every point) lowers your rate even further. Ensure that you will stay in the house long enough to recuperate the upfront expenditure through the rate cut.

• **Discuss Adjustable-Rate Options** - Adjustable-rate mortgages (ARMs) often offer lower initial rates than fixed-rate mortgages, but the interest can increase over time. Given the risk, undertake in-depth talks with your lender to thoroughly understand and predict the terms and rate change effects during the loan's life.

Chapter 5: The Final Walkthrough & Closing

Conducting a Final Walkthrough

Before the scheduled closing date, buyers and their agents should conduct a final walkthrough of the property. The purpose of the walkthrough is to confirm that all agreed-upon repairs have been completed, no additional damage has occurred, and the house is in a suitable condition for moving in based on the terms of the contract. During this inspection, certain key items are typically examined. These include checking for visible damage such as cracks, leaks, or flaws in walls, ceilings, and appliances, while plumbing and electrical systems can be checked by running faucets, flushing toilets, and turning on lights. Outside the property, buyers should also inspect the exterior for any noticeable damage, and confirm the presence of agreed-upon features such as sheds or fences.

To ensure a successful walkthrough, thoroughness is crucial. Every room, system, and item outlined in the contract should be checked carefully to avoid oversights. A checklist can be a helpful tool to track all items being inspected. In the event that any issues are discovered during the walkthrough, additional negotiations between the buyer and seller may be necessary to facilitate credits or repairs before the closing process can proceed. Buyers or their real estate agent should promptly inform their attorney of any major concerns identified during the inspection to facilitate the necessary follow-up actions.

Key points regarding the final walkthrough:

- **Be Thorough** - Check each room, system, and contract item meticulously. Rushing can lead to oversights.
- **Use a Checklist** - List all components to check so that they may be easily tracked during the comprehensive inspection.
- **Prepare to Negotiate** - If any faults are discovered, more buyer/seller negotiations on credits or fixes may be required

before closing can occur. Inform your attorney of any serious difficulties soon away to support the following actions.

In my experience as a buyer's agent, most final walkthroughs proceed relatively smoothly with no major property changes since the initial purchase agreement. However, issues like water leaks, leftover seller possessions or removed agreed-upon items may arise on occasion. Your agent should contact the seller's agent immediately regarding any issues to resolve before closing.

Preparing for a Smooth Closing Process

Preparing ahead of time is key to a successful real estate closing. Rather than rushing at the last minute, gather all necessary documents early. Items like a valid ID, a cashier's check for closing or down payment costs, and proof of homeowner's insurance are commonly required. Be prepared to provide any additional paperwork requested by your lender, title company, or attorney.

Carefully review the closing costs by examining the closing disclosure statement, typically provided by the title company or attorney, a day or two before signing. Take the time to go through each item on the sheet attentively, asking for clarification from your lender or attorney on any items that are unclear. Have the precise final closing dollar amount ready for payment in the form of a certified check or wire transfer.

Expect to sign several documents during the closing. Review all paperwork, including the closing statement, promissory note, deed of trust, and others. While your attorney will guide you through the documents, make sure to read them thoroughly to comprehend your obligations and address any queries before signing.

Obtain copies of all documents for your records before you leave. Being well-prepared, with all necessary documents and funds in order for signing, will ensure a seamless closing process. Once everything is in place, you'll officially become a new homeowner, ready to receive the keys to your new home!

Tips for a Stress-Free Move

Now that the closing process is complete and you have the keys to your new home, it's time to start moving in! Effective planning and preparation can help ensure a seamless transition. Here's a helpful checklist to guide you through the moving process:

- **Create a Realistic Moving Budget** - List all projected expenditures for truck rental, movers, and supplies. Sticking to your budget minimizes unexpected expenses.
- **Declutter First** - Before packing, get rid of any stuff you no longer need. This saves room and reduces your traveling burden.
- **Pack Strategically** - Use strong boxes and covers to secure your possessions. Label boxes by room to facilitate unloading later.
- **Mindfully Load, Transport and Unpack** - Load the truck's heaviest stuff first, with firmly stacked, secure crates. Unpack boxes when you arrive at your new house and place them in their proper places.
- **Hire Help if Needed** - If you don't have time or energy, full-service movers can handle everything from packing to transport to unloading. If you're on a tight budget, renting only a truck and a few buddies to help with the rest can help significantly.
- **Take Regular Breaks** - Pace yourself by taking regular pauses for food, drink, and relaxation. Moving involves both practical and emotional hardship. Self-care keeps you nourished and focused.

Careful preparation and planning will ensure your move goes smoothly. Stay organized with checklists and label your boxes by room. Remember to schedule regular breaks to stay energized. If hiring movers or using friends to help, show gratitude by providing food and celebrations afterwards! Focus on the excitement of this new chapter. Embrace fully the special memories you will create in your first home.

Chapter 6: Owning With Ease

First Projects to Tackle

Now that you've finished moving in and you're excited to get settled into your new place, it's a good idea to take a moment to tackle some important tasks before unpacking everything. This will help ensure that your new home is safe, enjoyable, and ready for you to make it your own as you step into the role of a new homeowner. This is your chance to kick off some initial projects that will enhance safety, cleanliness, and comfort in your new space.

Enhance Security- Having peace of mind is crucial for feeling safe, happy, and at ease in your new home. Work with a locksmith to install new locks that limit access to you and your family/occupants exclusively. Also, evaluate smoke detectors, alarms, and infrastructure integrity, and upgrade or replace anything that is required.

Conduct a Thorough Cleaning- Deep clean all rooms using your preferred products or pay a professional to do a comprehensive house cleaning before you move in. Fresh backdrops encourage new beginnings.

Attend to Repairs and Personalization- Take note of any damaged walls, drips, or peelings that require fresh coats of paint in colors of your choice. Install preferred furniture, photographs, and other décor to express your own individuality. Make the place your personal refuge.

Ongoing Maintenance and More

Budgeting for Ongoing Homeownership Costs

To avoid any financial surprises, it can be helpful as a new homeowner to set up a budget for your monthly housing expenses. Some things to consider:

- **Mortgage Payment**: Likely your largest monthly cost which includes principal, interest, taxes, and insurance (PITI).

- **Property Taxes**: If they're not already included in your mortgage payment, these are typically billed once or twice a year, depending on the area. These support communal resources like schools and parks.

- **Homeowner Insurance**: This typically covers damage from fires, theft, and natural disasters. Shop around for the best prices.

- **Maintenance and Repairs**: This covers appliance repair, yard work, and other upkeep tasks. Factor in more money as your house gets older.

- **Utilities**: Your electricity, water, and garbage collection costs will vary depending on your home's size and usage, but they're expenses that you will incur on a regular basis.

Budget for occasional big-ticket items such as:

- **Home Improvements:** These typically increase property value, but can be expensive. Prioritize improvements that fit within your budget.

- **Emergency Repairs:** Allocate funds specifically for unexpected issues that may arise and require immediate attention.

Other budgeting best practices:

- Estimate costs realistically, without underestimating.
- Build in flexibility for unexpected expenditures.
- Review and adapt as circumstances change. Shop around for the best rates on all services.
- Learning basic home repair skills to economize fixes.

Building Equity Over Time

A significant advantage of homeownership is the chance to accumulate equity, which is the difference between your home's market value and the amount owed on your mortgage loan. As your mortgage debt decreases, your equity increases. Here are some equity-building tips:

- Pay on time - Making monthly mortgage payments on time is critical for building equity.
- Add extra principal payments when possible - Even small amounts help pay off the principal faster.
- Choose a shorter mortgage term - Increased monthly payments are mitigated by quicker equity growth.
- Install energy-efficient upgrades - This reduces utility expenditures and increases a home's value.
- Refresh with cosmetic improvements - Fresh paint, flooring, carpets, and other features increase buyer appeal.
- Renovate or upgrade gradually - Targeted remodels within your budget can boost value.
- Maintain curb appeal - A well-kept yard can boost property value.

Additional factors impacting home values and equity growth include:

- Location - Desirable places usually appreciate quicker.
- Condition - Well-maintained properties attract higher sales prices.
- Market cycles - Seller's marketplaces provide greater sales prices.

Building equity gives you more financial options. The more equity you have, the more money you can borrow against your home if needed, for example with a home equity loan. Having equity also means you will make more money when you eventually sell the home. Keep making payments on time and make smart upgrades over time. Doing this will help your home become more valuable so your equity grows.

Easy Home Maintenance Checklist

Staying on top of home maintenance doesn't have to be overwhelming. Use this general checklist to remember key tasks, adjusting to fit your specific needs:

Daily

- Make beds
- Load/unload dishes
- Wipe counters
- Take out trash
- Tidy up clutter
- Sweep floors

- Water plants
- Turn off unused lights

Weekly

- Clean bathrooms/kitchen
- Sweep/vacuum
- Dust furniture
- Change linens if needed
- Take out recyclables
- Grocery shop/meal prep

Quarterly

- Clean windows/screens
- Inspect fire extinguisher
- Check water pressure
- Test sump pump
- Clean gutters

Annually

- Service HVAC system
- Clean chimney/fireplace
- Pump septic tank (if needed)

- Inspect water heater

- Replace air filters

Additional Helpful Tips:

- Use a log to track completed tasks

- Hire pros for complex maintenance

- Address issues like leaks quickly before they worsen

- Assign chores to family members

- Invest in quality cleaning supplies

- Keep your home organized for easier cleaning

- Let fresh air in to prevent moisture buildup

Routine walkthroughs make upkeep much simpler. Handle small fixes promptly to prevent big problems down the road.

Key Terms

1. **Adjustable-Rate Mortgage (ARM)** – A type of mortgage loan with an interest rate that can change periodically based on market conditions, typically starting with a fixed rate for an initial period before becoming adjustable. ARMs often have lower initial interest rates than fixed-rate mortgages, but the rate and monthly payments can fluctuate over time, potentially increasing the borrower's costs.

2. **Appraisal** – An estimate of the current market value of a home by a licensed appraiser that lenders use to determine loan amounts.
3. **Attorney Review Period** – A specific period after the signing of a real estate contract during which the parties can have their attorneys review and approve the terms of the agreement and suggest modifications if necessary. (More common in real estate transactions in states such as New Jersey and Illinois, e.g.)
4. **Buyer Representation** – The contractual relationship between a buyer and a real estate agent, where the agent represents the buyer's interests in the purchase of a property, provides guidance, conducts property searches, negotiates on behalf of the buyer, and ensures their best interests are protected throughout the transaction.
5. **Comparative Property Analysis (CMA)** – An evaluation of similar properties in the same area to determine a property's fair market value based on factors such as size, location, features, and recent sales prices.
6. **Closing Costs** – Fees paid to finalize the property purchase transaction, including lender origination fees, title insurance, recording fees, and more.
7. **Closing Disclosure Statement** – A document provided to the borrower before closing on a mortgage loan that outlines the final terms and costs of the loan, including loan amount, interest rate, closing costs, and any other fees associated with the transaction. It ensures transparency and helps borrowers understand the financial details of the loan before finalizing the deal.
8. **Condominium** – A residential unit within a larger complex or building where individuals own their unit and then co-own shared resources like lobbies or pools through monthly condo association fees.

9. **Consumer Financial Protection Bureau (CFPB)** – A federal agency responsible for regulating and enforcing consumer protection laws in the financial sector. Its primary focus is to ensure fair treatment for consumers in financial
10. **Conventional Loan** – A type of mortgage loan not insured or guaranteed by a government entity, such as the FHA or VA, typically offered by private lenders. Conventional loans often have stricter credit and down payment requirements compared to government-backed loans and may have fixed or adjustable interest rates.
11. **Cooperative Housing** – A form of residential ownership where residents collectively own and manage the property through a corporation.
12. **Credit Builder Loan** – A type of loan designed to help individuals establish or improve their credit history by borrowing a small amount of money, making regular payments, and demonstrating responsible credit behavior to boost their credit score.
13. **Credit Reporting Agencies** – Companies that collect, track, and report individuals' credit information to lenders and other authorized parties, generating credit reports and credit scores based on factors such as payment history, credit accounts, inquiries, and public records. Notable credit reporting agencies include Equifax, Experian, and TransUnion.
14. **Credit Score** – A number ranging from 300-850 estimating an individual's credit risk level determined by payment history, amounts owed, types of credit used, and other factors.
15. **Debt-to-Income Ratio** – The percentage of gross monthly income allocated towards paying debts calculated by lenders when qualifying borrowers.
16. **Discount Points** – Fees paid to a lender at closing in exchange for a lower interest rate on a mortgage, allowing borrowers to reduce their monthly mortgage payments over the life of the loan in exchange for an upfront cost.

17. **Down Payment** – The upfront percentage of the total purchase price borrowed for a home is put towards the buyer's cost. Typically, 10-20% or less, depending on the type of loan.
18. **Earnest Money** – An initial deposit submitted with an offer to show the seller a buyer's good faith to fulfill the terms of the purchase contract. Held in escrow until closing.
19. **Escrow** – A neutral third-party account holding buyer and seller funds for transaction fees and closing costs until the sale is finalized.
20. **Exclusive Buyer Representation** – Buyer representation is taken further by agreeing that only one specific agent, not competing agents, solely assists the buyer.
21. **Fair Housing** – Federal and state laws prohibit discrimination in purchasing, selling, or renting housing based on race, color, national origin, religion, sex, handicap, or familial status.
22. **FHA Loan** – Mortgage loans backed by the Federal Housing Administration, designed to make homeownership more accessible to low and moderate-income individuals by offering lower down payment requirements and more flexible qualification criteria than conventional loans. FHA loans are insured by the government, providing lenders with greater security, which allows them to offer loans to borrowers who may not qualify for conventional financing.
23. **Final Walkthrough** – A last inspection of the property conducted by the buyer before closing to ensure that the property is in the expected condition, any agreed-upon repairs have been made, and that no unexpected issues have arisen since the initial inspection. It allows the buyer to confirm that the property is in the same state as when the offer was accepted.
24. **Fixed-rate Mortgage** – A home loan with an interest rate remaining constant over the full loan term, commonly 15 or 30 years.

25. **For Sale by Owner (FSBO)** – When a home seller markets and sells their home themselves without enlisting a real estate agent's representation or listings access.
26. **Foreclosure** – The legal process where a lender takes ownership of a property after the borrower defaults on the mortgage and sells it to recover loan losses.
27. **Home Inspection** – A thorough inspection of the physical condition of a home by a professional identifying any code violations, damage, or needed repairs before purchase.
28. **Home Warranty** – An optional insurance policy that pays for repairs or replacement costs of major home systems and appliances that unexpectedly break down over a specified coverage period.
29. **Homeowner Insurance** - A type of property insurance that provides coverage for damage or loss to a home and its contents, as well as liability coverage for accidents that may occur on the property.
30. **Homeowners Association (HOA)** – An organization in certain neighborhoods or communities that mandates rules and collects monthly dues to maintain amenities or common areas.
31. **Lead-Based Paint Disclosure** – Disclosure of lead present within homes painted before 1978 gave health concerns, especially among small children, stemming from lead exposure, which can impair brain development.
32. **Licensed Home Inspector** – A professional who is certified and authorized to conduct inspections of residential properties to assess their condition and identify any potential issues or problems.
33. **Listing Types** – Different methods of selling a property, including Regular Sale, Private Network, Short Sale, Foreclosure, For Sale by Owner (FSBO), and New Construction.
34. **Loan Officer** – A financial professional who assists borrowers in the mortgage application process, evaluates their financial

situation, helps them choose the right loan product, and guides them through the loan approval process.
35. **Market Conditions** – The overall state of the real estate market, which can be categorized as a Buyer's Market (favoring buyers) or Seller's Market (favoring sellers).
36. **MLS – Multiple Listing Service** – The centralized regional database of properties listed for sale is accessible by subscribing real estate agents representing buyers and sellers.
37. **Mortgage Broker** – An adviser consolidating rates from multiple lenders to secure a borrower the best financing terms on a home loan. They facilitate the loan process from application to closing.
38. **Mortgage Calculator** – Tools that help individuals estimate their potential monthly mortgage payments based on factors such as loan amount, interest rate, and term length.
39. **Mold Disclosure** – Paperwork denoting if the seller ever encountered mold issues within a dwelling given moisture enables microscopic spores triggering allergies and long-term respiratory risks if left unchecked.
40. **Pre-Approval** – A letter indicating the loan amount and terms a lender will offer a prospective homebuyer contingent on appraisal, etc.
41. **Prequalification** – A non-binding estimate of the home loan size and conditions a buyer may qualify for based on verbal financials.
42. **Principal** – The amount borrowed for the home purchase is separate from interest paid over the total mortgage loan repayment term.
43. **Property Disclosures** – Documents detailing any known defects present in a home for ethical disclosure to buyers from sellers transparently sharing pertinent property history.
44. **Property Taxes** – Annual taxes levied by local government against homeowners are typically tied to home values used for funding public services.

45. **Purchase Agreement** - The contract specifying all terms and conditions between the buyer and seller of a residential property transaction, including contingencies.
46. **Radon Disclosure** – Specific documentation on whether a home has undergone radon inspection and mitigation given high radon levels pose serious health hazards yet stand asymptomatic and undetectable otherwise.
47. **Real Estate Agent** – A licensed professional who assists buyers and sellers in real estate transactions, guiding them through the buying and selling process.
48. **Real Estate Attorney** – A licensed professional specializing in real estate law who provides legal advice and guidance during property transactions, ensuring all legal aspects are handled correctly.
49. **Realtor®** – A real estate professional who is an active member of the National Association of Realtors® (NAR). The term Realtor® is a registered trademark that can only be used by individuals who have completed the required education, subscribe to the Realtor® Code of Ethics, and are members of their local Realtor® association as well as the state and national associations.
50. **Seller Concessions** – Credits issued by home sellers at closing towards a buyer's closing costs or other expenses as an incentive to complete the sale.
51. **Short Sale** – When the lender agrees to allow a financially struggling borrower to sell their home for less than the loan balance owed.
52. **Single Family Home** – A standalone residential property not sharing any walls or resources held under single ownership.
53. **Smart Home Upgrades** – Technological enhancements made to a property to increase convenience, security, energy efficiency, and connectivity through the integration of smart home devices and systems, such as smart thermostats, door

locks, lighting, security cameras, and voice-activated assistants.
54. **Title Company** – A business entity that specializes in conducting title searches, issuing title insurance, and facilitating the closing process in real estate transactions.
55. **Title Insurance** – An insurance policy protecting home buyers from legal issues or claims challenging their legal ownership rights to the property after purchase.
56. **Townhome** – Similar to condos, townhomes denote multiple attached housing units where owners hold title to their property while exterior walls and roofs are handled collectively.
57. **USDA Loan** – Mortgage loans provided by the United States Department of Agriculture for rural homebuyers with low to moderate incomes.
58. **VA Loan** – A mortgage loan guaranteed by the Department of Veterans Affairs (VA) that is available to eligible service members, veterans, and their families. VA loans typically offer favorable terms, including no down payment or mortgage insurance requirement, competitive interest rates, and flexible qualification criteria, making homeownership more accessible to those who have served in the military.

Navigating Real Estate Transactions Across the 50 States

Real estate transactions follow different legal processes across the 50 states when it comes to working with real estate agents, utilizing attorneys, conducting closings, handling FSBO sales, and meeting other state-level requirements.

While core elements of buying and selling property remain similar nationwide, key differences related to regulations, contracts, and customs do exist from state to state. For example, some states require attorney representation for all housing transactions, while others allow DIY options without legal counsel. Several states mandate seller disclosures detailing home defects, while others impose no such requirements. There is also variation around topics like earnest money policies, title insurance norms, broker fiduciary duties and more based on distinct state laws.

Given this patchwork of state-by-state variation, it is essential that home buyers and sellers educate themselves on practices, disclosures, regulations and laws specific to their area prior to entering into any real estate transaction. Legal and procedural differences abound between states when transacting property sales. Taking time to research and understand your rights and responsibilities within your exact city, county and state will help real estate consumers make informed decisions while ensuring full compliance through what can be a complex legal and financial process.

Below is a detailed overview of how real estate transactions differ across the 50 states when it comes to working with agents, attorneys, closings, FSBO properties, and other legal requirements.

Alabama

- No law requires a buyer's agent
- Attorneys typically not involved in real estate transactions
- Closings handled by title company or mortgage lender
- The growing popularity of FSBO requires buyers to represent their interests

Alaska

- Remote location limits agent options, so most act as dual agents
- Lawyers commonly used to review property disclosures

- Closings take place at the title company office
- For FSBO sales, the standard purchase agreement used

Arizona

- Buyer's agents are optional but recommended
- Attorneys draft contracts but not closing docs
- The escrow company handles closing logistics
- Large FSBO market using standard forms

Arkansas

- No requirement for the buyer's agent
- Real estate attorneys are less common
- Closings are done at the title company office
- FSBO properties utilize offer/acceptance contract

California

- No mandated buyer's agent, but very common
- Attorney representation heavily advised
- The escrow company handles closing details
- Disclosures & agents critical for FSBO deals

Colorado

- Buyer's agents optional
- Lawyer reviews but typically not at closing
- The title company conducts the closing
- FSBO is very popular with standardized forms

Connecticut

- No requisite buyer's agent
- An attorney often reviews documents

- The attorney typically supervises the closing
- FSBO is uncommon due to closing complexity

Delaware

- Most use buyer's agent
- An attorney is usually part of the process
- Closings are done at the title company
- FSBO is uncommon, given disclosure laws

Florida

- No mandate for the buyer's agent
- Real estate lawyers are typically not needed
- Closings handled by the title company
- Large FSBO market using standard forms

Georgia

- Agents and attorneys are both common
- Attorney attendance at closing varies
- Closings done at a title company or lender
- Specific power of attorney required for FSBO

Hawaii

- Single agents often represent both sides
- Lawyer reviews documents as standard
- Escrow company runs closing
- Strict FSBO disclosures required

Idaho

- No required buyer's agent
- Attorney involvement uncommon

- The title company handles the closing
- Disclosure form used for most FSBO

Illinois

- No mandate for buyer's representation
- Real estate attorneys permitted at closing
- Closings are done at title companies, typically
- The attorney recommended an FSBO contract

Indiana

- Most utilize buyer's agent
- An attorney can review the purchase agreement
- Title company administers closing docs
- FSBO utilizes standardized purchase forms

Iowa

- Exclusive buyer's agent prevails
- Real estate lawyers can attend the closing
- Separate closing company common
- Attorneys more involved with FSBO deals

Kansas

- Buyer's agents are increasingly popular
- Real estate attorneys are not typical
- Closings handled by the title company
- Specific power of attorney common for FSBO

Kentucky

- Single-agent often represents both parties
- Attorney involvement is less prevalent

- Title company runs closing appointments
- FSBO disclosure form utilized

Louisiana

- Mandatory buyer's agent disclosure
- Real estate lawyer involvement varies
- Separate notaries handle closings
- Attorney recommended for FSBO deals

Maine

- Buyer's agent required for MLS homes
- Attorney representation frequently advised
- Closings take place at the title company
- Specific power of attorney for FSBO

Maryland

- No required buyer's agent
- Real estate attorneys may attend the closing
- The settlement agent oversees the closing
- Strict FSBO disclosures apply.

Massachusetts

- Buyer's agent prevalence growing
- Mandatory attorney involvement
- The attorney runs the closing appointment
- Specific FSBO purchase contract

Michigan

- Exclusive buyer's agency agreements increasing
- Real estate attorneys permitted at closing

- The title insurance company handles the closing
- Standard purchase agreement for FSBO

Minnesota

- Typical to hire a buyer's agent
- Lawyer representation dependent on deal complexity
- A separate closing company or attorney office is used
- FSBO paperwork support offered by the state

Mississippi

- Buyer's agent optional for MLS listings
- Attorney representation is less widespread
- A title company facilitates the closing
- FSBO sales commonly use standardized forms

Missouri

- No mandatory buyer's agent
- Real estate attorney usage diverges
- A separate title company oversees the closing
- Power of attorney advised for FSBO deals

Montana

- Buyer's agent recommended not required
- Attorney representation is less prevalent
- Title company coordinates closing
- FSBO utilizes residential sales contract

Nebraska

- The buyer's agent is not legally mandated
- Real estate attorneys can be involved

- The title company runs the closing process
- FSBO advised to use standard contracts

Nevada

- Lawyer representation is quite common
- The title company facilitates the closing process
- FSBO disclosures specifically outlined

New Hampshire

- Buyer's agent suggested best practice
- Real estate attorney involvement varies
- The title company handles closing details
- FSBOs are advised to consult forms/regulations

New Jersey

- The buyer's agent recommended
- Mandatory attorney involvement
- The attorney supervises the closing appointment
- Standardized FSBO contracts exist

New Mexico

- Exclusive buyer's agency rare
- Real estate attorneys may be used
- The title company administers the closing process
- FSBOs leverage standard documents

New York

- The buyer's agent can be used
- Attorney participation is relatively common
- Closing takes place at the attorney's office

- Power of attorney advised for FSBO

North Carolina

- No requirement for buyer's representation
- Real estate attorneys are sometimes involved
- The title company facilitates the closing process
- Specific FSBO disclosures and forms required

North Dakota

- Buyer's agent not mandated
- Real estate attorney involvement varies
- The title company conducts the closing
- FSBO sales use typical contracts

Ohio

- Buyer's agent optional
- Attorney representation rarer
- A title company facilitates the closing
- FSBO property disclosures mandated

Oklahoma

- No mandate for the buyer's agent
- Attorney roles are typically limited
- The title company handles the closing
- FSBOs must provide purchase documents

Oregon

- Mandatory buyer's agent in MLS listings
- A lawyer can review the purchase agreement
- Title company runs closing

- FSBO sales are regulated by disclosure

Pennsylvania

- Buyer's agent prevalent practice
- Lawyer roles dependent on deal intricacy
- A title company facilitates the closing
- FSBO advised thoroughly reading guidelines

Rhode Island

- The buyer's agent recommended
- An attorney may be present at closing
- The title company runs a closing process
- FSBO transactions use set paperwork

South Carolina

- Single-agent often represents both parties
- Attorney participation infrequent
- The title company handles the closing
- FSBO sales are strictly regulated by form

South Dakota

- Buyer's representation is not legally mandated
- Attorney attendance at closing discretionary
- The title company oversees closing processes
- Standardized contracts used in FSBO sales

Tennessee

- No buyer's agent requirement
- Attorney involvement is less common
- The title company handles the closing

- FSBO disclosures protect transparency

Texas

- Buyer's representation optional
- Attorneys less frequently appear
- The title company oversees closing appointments
- FSBO contractual standards enforced

Utah

- Exclusive buyer's agency more widespread
- Attorney involvement dictated by deal complexity
- The title company runs a closing appointment
- FSBO transactions utilize specific forms

Vermont

- Buyer's agent commonly leveraged
- Attorney roles dependent on specifics
- The title company handles closing logistics
- Disclosures regulate FSBO sales

Virginia

- No mandate for buyer's representation
- Attorney participation varies
- The settlement agent oversees the closing
- FSBO property condition disclosures are required

Washington

- Buyer's agency agreements are typical
- The attorney reviews major documentation
- The escrow company conducts the closing

- FSBO sales utilize specific forms

West Virginia

- The buyer's agent is not legally required
- Attorney presence depends on the deal
- The settlement firm handles the closing
- FSBO documentation regulates transparency

Wisconsin

- Stricter buyer's agency laws
- Real estate attorneys are sometimes involved
- Third-party closer administers process
- FSBO transactions use set paperwork

Wyoming

- Buyer's agentless strictly enforced
- Attorney involvement depends on specifics
- The title company runs a closing appointment

Note that the above information was verified at the time of this writing and is subject to change.

<*-END-*>

DISCLAIMER

Legal Disclosure: The information provided in this book is for educational and informational purposes only. It is not intended as legal or investment advice or professional guidance. Readers are encouraged to consult with licensed real estate professionals, financial advisors, and legal experts for specific advice tailored to their individual circumstances. The author, as a licensed real estate professional, shares knowledge and insights based on experience and research, but makes no guarantees regarding the accuracy, completeness, or applicability of the information provided. The author and publisher shall not be held liable for any losses, damages, or legal repercussions resulting from the use or interpretation of the information contained in this book. Any reliance on the material presented is at the reader's own risk.

www.ingramcontent.com/pod-product-compliance
Lightning Source LLC
Chambersburg PA
CBHW070357230526
45471CB00006B/2615